Dustin Pedroia

By Jon M. Fishman

AMAZING ATHLETES

Lerner Publications • Minneapolis

Lerner Publications Company
A division of Lerner Publishing Group, Inc.
241 First Avenue North
Minneapolis, MN 55401 USA

For reading levels and more information, look up this title at www.lernerbooks.com.

Library of Congress Cataloging-in-Publication Data

The Cataloging-in-Publication Data for *Dustin Pedroia* is on file at the Library of Congress.
ISBN: 978–1–4677–5743-0 (lib. bdg.)
ISBN: 978-1-4677-6054-6 (pbk.)
ISBN: 978–1–4677–6211-3 (EB pdf)

Manufactured in the United States of America
1 – BP – 12/31/14

TABLE OF CONTENTS

Dustin Pedroia gets a hit during the 2013 World Series.

WORLD SERIES STAR

Boston Red Sox second baseman Dustin Pedroia stood near first base. He had just smashed a **line drive** to the outfield. His eyes were glued to St. Louis Cardinals pitcher Adam Wainwright. Dustin was watching for a chance to move to second.

The Red Sox and the Cardinals were playing the first game of the 2013 World Series. It was at Fenway Park in Boston on October 23. The first team to win four games in the series would be the champion of Major League Baseball (MLB). The stakes were high. But Dustin stayed calm. He had helped the Red Sox win the World Series in 2007. His teammates looked to him as a leader.

Fenway Park is the oldest MLB ballpark still in use. It was built in 1912.

Fans watch the Red Sox take on the Cardinals during Game 1 of the 2013 World Series at Fenway Park.

Boston **designated hitter** David Ortiz came to bat next. He whacked the ball onto the ground. The Cardinals flipped the ball to second base before Dustin could get there. He was called out. But Boston **manager** John Farrell came out of the **dugout** to argue the call. He thought the Cardinals had dropped the ball before touching second base. The **umpires** agreed. Dustin was safe!

Pete Kozma *(right)* drops the ball as Dustin slides into second base.

Next up was first baseman Mike Napoli. He crushed the ball to the outfield for a **double**. Dustin and two teammates came roaring home to score. Boston had the lead, 3–0.

Dustin *(center)* urges David Ortiz to slide as he runs home on a hit by Mike Napoli.

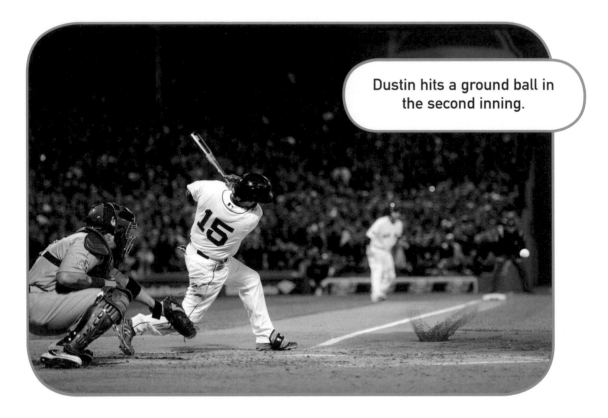

Dustin hits a ground ball in the second inning.

Dustin came to bat again in the second inning. The bases were loaded. He swung and sent the ball bouncing along the ground. Red Sox **shortstop** Stephen Drew ran home. Dustin's hit made the score 4–0. Dustin got on base again in the seventh inning. When Ortiz hit a home run, Dustin scored.

Boston won the game, 8–1. It was a huge win. But Dustin knew the Cardinals would keep fighting for the championship, just as the Red Sox would. "Both teams have played their tails off this year to get to this point," he said. The 2013 World Series was just getting started.

Dustin runs the bases in the seventh inning.

Dustin grew up in Woodland, California. Woodland is near the city of Sacramento.

A WINNING FAMILY

Dustin Luis Pedroia was born on August 17, 1983, in Woodland, California. He lived there with his parents and older brother, Brett.

Dustin was a baseball player from the beginning. Almost as soon as he could walk, he began swinging a tiny wooden bat. He swung the bat at all kinds of things—tin foil, Ping-Pong balls, anything that looked round.

But the young slugger soon learned that swinging belonged on the field. Dustin joined a T-ball league when he was four years old. His mother, Debbie, was the coach. Debbie was just five feet tall. But her height hadn't stopped her from playing sports in college. She taught her son that working hard is more important than size.

Dustin loves to play Ping-Pong. When he was young, he would fold up one end of a Ping-Pong table. That way, he could bounce the ball off the folded table and play by himself.

Like this boy, Dustin played T-ball when he was a child.

Debbie also taught her son how much fun it is to win. She never wanted to lose. Guy Pedroia, Dustin's father, watched his wife coach Dustin and his teammates on the T-ball field. "She was tough," Guy said. Debbie wanted her players to try hard and to win.

Guy Pedroia owns an auto repair and tire store called Valley Tire Center in Woodland. Guy bought the business in 1982.

Dustin's brother, Brett, hangs a Red Sox banner in the Pedroia family's auto repair shop.

Guy spent many hours with his sons practicing baseball. Dustin liked swinging a bat. But Guy knew that being able to catch and throw a ball was just as important as batting. He passed that lesson on to his son. Dustin often wanted his dad to pitch to him. Guy agreed, as long as Dustin spent just as much time practicing his fielding.

Dustin moved on to Little League baseball after T-ball. When he was 12 years old, his team won so many games that they almost made it to the Little League Baseball World Series.

In high school, Dustin enjoyed playing several sports, including football.

PROVING HIMSELF

In 1997, Dustin began his freshman year at Woodland High School. He played football and basketball as well as baseball. He worked hard to win no matter what sport he was playing.

Dustin became the freshman football team's quarterback. At five feet three inches tall, he was smaller than most of his teammates. His small size didn't stop him from being a good quarterback. But he was soon injured by a big hit. Dustin's ankle was badly broken. He had two surgeries.

Dustin decided to stop playing football and basketball. He wanted to stick with just one sport: baseball.

Dustin had just one worry as he was rushed from the football field to the hospital with a broken ankle: "I'll never be able to play baseball again."

Focusing on baseball paid off. Dustin could devote time to becoming better and better. His skills improved, and the competition noticed. Rob Bruno, the coach of a **rival** team, was impressed by Dustin's abilities. "[Dustin] was a 15-year-old who looked like a 13-year-old playing like an 18-year-old," Bruno said.

Dustin bloomed as a shortstop for Woodland. He had a **batting average** of .448. He also smacked 12 doubles, a **triple**, and two home runs during his sophomore year. Dustin was named the team's Most Valuable Player (MVP) at the end of the season. His hitting continued to improve. He finished his junior year with a .459 batting average.

Dustin *(front row center)* played shortstop for the Woodland Wolves baseball team.

Rob Rinaldi coached Dustin's baseball team at Woodland. Coach Rinaldi loved the way his young shortstop played the game. But he didn't think Dustin was tall enough to play in college or on an MLB team. He told the Pedroias what he thought.

Dustin walks with his mom, Debbie, at homecoming during his senior year at Woodland.

Dustin's mom believed in her son. "You just wait," Debbie told Rinaldi. "He's going to prove all of you wrong if somebody just gives him a chance."

Dustin was determined to succeed in baseball.

The next year, Dustin wanted to show Coach Rinaldi that he belonged in the big leagues. He batted .445. And he didn't strike out all season. Dustin was named Metro Player of the Year for the Sacramento area.

The Arizona State University Sun Devils baseball team plays at Packard Stadium in Tempe, Arizona.

SUN DEVIL

Dustin had shown that he was good enough to play college baseball. **Scouts** around the country took notice. Many schools showed interest in Dustin. He finally decided to attend Arizona State University (ASU). ASU had a great baseball team. The Sun Devils had won the college baseball national championship five times. And famous baseball players, including Barry Bonds, had attended the school.

Many athletes struggle during their first year at a new level. But Dustin took to the college game right away. His batting average for the 2002 season was .347. That was the fourth-best average on the team and the highest among freshmen.

Dustin gets a hit during a game in February 2003.

Dustin continued to improve as a shortstop. Here he throws the ball to make a play in 2004.

ASU gave Dustin a **scholarship**. But he wanted to give it back after his freshman year. He thought ASU should give the scholarship to a talented pitcher named Ben Thurmond. Dustin thought Ben would be a good addition to the Sun Devils.

When Dustin told his dad about his plan to return the scholarship, Guy agreed. The Pedroia family could still afford to pay for Dustin's school. And with both Dustin and Ben, the Sun Devils would be an even stronger team.

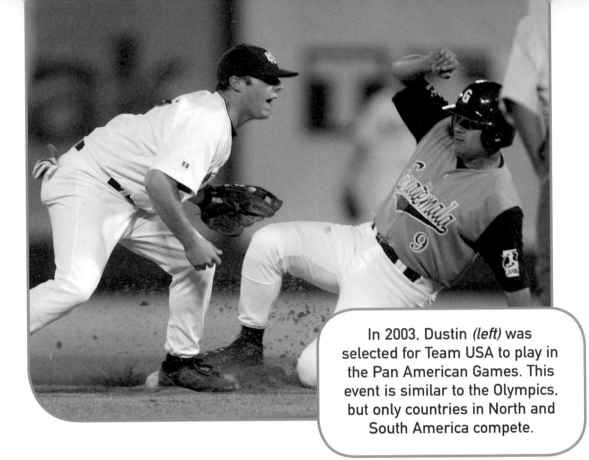

In 2003, Dustin *(left)* was selected for Team USA to play in the Pan American Games. This event is similar to the Olympics, but only countries in North and South America compete.

Dustin did everything he could to help his team win in 2003. He batted an incredible .404. He was named co-Player of the Year in his **conference**. He was also named the best defensive player in the country. All the fielding practice he had done with his dad had paid off. The small shortstop was known as one of the best college baseball players in the country.

After three great seasons at ASU, Dustin decided he wanted to play for a professional team. He joined the 2004 MLB **draft**. Some teams were worried that Dustin was too small to play professional baseball. But the Boston Red Sox disagreed. They snatched him with the 65th pick. Dustin was fired up. "I am pretty excited about being picked by Boston, and it is a dream come true to hear my name in the draft," he said. "It is kind of an unreal feeling."

Dustin started his career in the minor leagues. He played for the Pawtucket Red Sox from 2005 to 2006.

WORLD-BEATER

Boston wanted Dustin to get more practice before joining Boston full-time. Dustin spent the next three years playing for some of the Red Sox's **minor-league** teams. During this time, his coaches moved him from shortstop to second base. In 2006, Dustin got to play 31 games with the Red Sox. And in 2007, he finally joined the team for the whole season.

It took Dustin a while to feel comfortable with the Red Sox. His batting average after the first month was a weak .172. But he quickly picked up his game. He finished the year with a .317 batting average. Dustin had just one goal in mind. "The only thing I cared about was trying to help the team win," he said.

Dustin made his major-league debut in August 2006.

In 2007, Boston made it to the **playoffs**. And then they made it all the way to the World Series. They beat the Colorado Rockies in four games. Dustin and the Red Sox were MLB champions!

Dustin won the 2007 **Rookie** of the Year award in the American League (AL). And Dustin kept improving. In 2008, he hit .326 with 17 home runs. Dustin was named AL MVP. "It's unbelievable," he said.

Dustin celebrates after hitting a home run during the 2007 World Series.

Dustin signs autographs for fans before a game in 2013.

The Red Sox continued to win many games with Dustin's help. But they didn't get back to the World Series until 2013. After crushing the Cardinals in Game 1, the Red Sox won three of the next five games. Dustin was an MLB champion for the second time!

The Red Sox have won the World Series eight times: 1903, 1912, 1915, 1916, 1918, 2004, 2007, and 2013.

Dustin rides in the 2013 All-Star Parade with his wife, Kelli, and sons Dylan *(center)* and Cole *(right)*. A third son, Brooks, was born in June 2014.

By now, no one doubted Dustin based on his size. His mother had been right when her son was in high school. Dustin had proven the doubters wrong. He had become one of the best baseball players in the world. "He has been proving himself every day of his life," Debbie said. "That's what makes him who he is."

Selected Career Highlights

2014 Hit more than 30 doubles in a season
for the seventh time

2013 Helped Boston win the World Series
Named to the MLB All-Star Game for the
fourth time

2011 Finished seventh in the AL in batting
average (.307)

2010 Named to the MLB All-Star Game for the
third time

2009 Named to the MLB All-Star Game for the
second time

2008 Named to the MLB All-Star Game for the first time
Won the AL MVP award

2007 Helped Boston win the World Series
Named AL Rookie of the Year
Played a full season with Boston

2006 Called up to play 31 games with the Boston Red Sox

2004 Chosen by the Boston Red Sox in the MLB draft
Named ASU offensive MVP

2003 Named co-Player of the Year in ASU's conference
Set team and conference records with 34 doubles

2002 Set ASU freshman record for hits (82)
Named ASU defensive MVP

2001 Started school at ASU
Graduated from Woodland High School

2000 Named to the high school all-state team for the third time
Named Metro Player of the Year for the Sacramento area

1999 Named to the high school all-state team for the second time

1998 Named Woodland baseball team MVP
Named to the high school all-state baseball team

1997 Started at Woodland High School

Glossary

batting average: a number that describes how often a baseball player makes a base hit

conference: a group of sports teams that play one another

designated hitter: a player who bats in place of the pitcher and doesn't play in the field

double: a hit in which the batter is able to reach second base safely

draft: a yearly event in which professional teams take turns choosing new players from a selected group

dugout: the area on the side of a baseball field where the players sit

line drive: a batted ball that travels in a straight line

manager: the top coach on a baseball team

minor league: a group of teams where players improve their skills and prepare to advance to Major League Baseball

playoffs: a series of games played at the end of the season to determine a champion

rival: a team that often plays against another team

rookie: a player who is playing his or her first season in the league

scholarship: money given to a student by a school or another group to help pay for school

scouts: people who judge the abilities of athletes

shortstop: a baseball player who usually stands to the left of second base

triple: a hit in which the batter is able to reach third base safely

umpires: officials who makes sure players follow the rules at a sports event

Further Reading & Websites

Doeden, Matt. *The World Series: Baseball's Biggest Stage*. Minneapolis: Millbrook Press, 2014.

Kennedy, Mike, and Mark Stewart. *Long Ball: The Legend and Lore of the Home Run*. Minneapolis: Millbrook Press, 2006.

Savage, Jeff. *David Ortiz*. Minneapolis: Lerner Publications, 2015.

Major League Baseball: The Official Site
http://mlb.mlb.com/home
The official Major League Baseball website provides fans with game results, statistics, schedules, and biographies of players.

The Official Site of the Boston Red Sox
http://boston.redsox.mlb.com/index.jsp?c_id=bos
The official website of the Boston Red Sox includes the team schedule and game results, biographies of Dustin Pedroia and other players and coaches, and much more.

Sports Illustrated Kids
http://www.sikids.com
The *Sports Illustrated Kids* website covers all sports, including baseball.

Index

Photo Acknowledgments

The images in this book are used with the permission of: © Jim Rogash/Getty Images, p. 4; © Rob Tringali/MLB Photos via Getty Images, p. 5; © Elsa/Getty Images, pp. 6, 9; © Bill Greene/The Boston Globe via Getty Images, p. 7; © Michael Ivins/Boston Red Sox/Getty Images, p. 8; © Photoquest/Dreamstime.com, p. 10; © iStockphoto.com/dwall817, p. 11; © Robert Durell/San Francisco Chronicle/CORBIS, p. 12; © iStockphoto.com/Terry J Alcorn, p. 14; Seth Poppel Yearbook Library, pp. 16, 17, 18; © Mark J. Rebilas/USA TODAY Sports, p. 19; © Rick Scuteri/USA TODAY Sports, p. 20; © Arizona State/Collegiate Images/Getty Images, p. 21; Jim Young/Reuters/Newscom, p. 22; AP Photo/Mike Janes/Four Seam Images, p. 24; © Otto Greule Jr/agency/Getty Images, p. 25; © Rich Pilling/MLB Photos via Getty Images, p. 26; © Al Messerschmidt/Getty Images, p. 27; © Thomas Levinson/MLB Photos via Getty Images, p. 28; © Rich Gangon/Getty Images, p. 29.

Front cover: © Jim Rogash/Getty Images.

Main body text set in Caecilia LT Std 55 Roman 16/28.
Typeface provided by Adobe Systems.